TABLE OF CONTENTS

Workbook Answers 4
Reading: Literature 4
Reading: Informational 6
Reading: Foundational Skills 8
Writing 9
Language 10
Practice Test Answers 15
Practice Test #1 15
Answers and Explanations 15
Practice Test #2 19
Answers and Explanations 19
Online Resources 24

Workbook Answers

Reading: Literature

Living on a Ranch

1. C - The Bar M Bar Ranch is in Laramie, Wyoming
2. D - Marcus uses whistles and calls.
3. B - Marcus enjoys working with the sheep.
4. A - Everyone has a job on a ranch.
5. C - She is in charge of the household and bills.
6. B - Working and living on a ranch is a full time job.
7. B - People who work on a ranch owned by someone else.
8. A - They all help with chores on the ranch.

Geocaching

1. C - He always has fun when he was with Tommy and Mr. Jones.
2. A - The GPS was only accurate to 15 feet.
3. C - wool socks, hiking boots, and a backpack
4. A - Geocaching is a treasure hunt for small containers using GPS coordinates.
5. B - small items or toys to trade
6. D - Yes, Tommy teaches Sam about marking off a search area.
7. B - two friends going Geocaching with Mr. Jones
8. D - a hiding place

Dance Class

1. A - They want to learn to dance.
2. C - Jillian loves ballet, and Samantha loves tap.
3. D - Both classrooms have wooden floors and mirrors.
4. C - a classical type of dance
5. D - a bar on the wall for stretching
6. B - how much the sisters loved dance

Island Ponies

1. C - Assateague horses and Chincoteague ponies are the same breed of horse.
2. B - someone who watches
3. D - They both have a National Park.
4. A - two herds of horses on Assateague Island
5. B - The Chincoteague ponies are given veterinary care.
6. D - The reader might think the firefighters were just being mean to the ponies.

Katie's Journal

1. A - Katie having a fight with her friend Sandy.
2. B - strained
3. C - The reader wouldn't know that the fight had been resolved.
4. A - The reader would not be able to know Katie's thoughts.
5. A - Katie was angry, but she became calm.
6. C - Even though they weren't speaking, Katie and Sandy still found a way to be mean in science.

An Artist Thinking BIG

1. D - Gutzon Borglum
2. A - Mount Rushmore is the most famous of the three mountain carvings.
3. B - All three carvings were finished by someone other than the original artist.
4. B - huge
5. A - three mountain carvings and the artist that connects them
6. D - Crazy Horse is the biggest and isn't finished yet.

The Disappearing Hair Ribbons

1. B - someone who is thought to be guilty
2. A - Pilar is upset.
3. B - Pilar's ribbons went missing before Rosa agreed to help.
4. A - Rosa searched Riley's habitat after she agreed to help.
5. A - Stinky climbed in Pilar's boot after Rosa agreed to help.
6. C - Pilar and Rosa were neighborhood detectives.

Reading: Informational

Animals of Yellowstone

1. D - He wanted to know where to look for the animals.
2. A - South Entrance and West Thumb
3. B - Elk
4. C - More animals live in forests and meadows.
5. D - an animal's home area
6. B - The wolves have the smallest population.

A Day in the City

1. D - subway
2. C - Which subway lines would you take to get to the National Archives?
3. B - They enjoy doing things together.
4. C - The White House and the National Air and Space Museum
5. A - Definition 1. - A sheet arranging information into columns or tabs
6. A - It is only on one subway line.

Family Names

1. C - to explain family names based on occupation
2. A - to move people or things
3. D - definitions and origins of occupational words
4. B - was a chef.
5. A - Fletcher and Bender
6. C - last Name

Meteor Watching

1. C - The Perseid meteor shower is a favorite.
2. A - It only happens in August.
3. C - scattered fragments of rock

4. D - The Earth takes one year to orbit the sun, and the comet takes 135 years to orbit the sun.
5. B - People enjoy watching the shower because it happens in the summer.
6. B - average

Reading: Foundational Skills

Root Words

1. cycle
2. comfort
3. bio
4. fill
5. arrange

Prefixes

1. *ir-* C: lacking responsibility
2. *anti-* B: a liquid used to keep other liquids from freezing
3. *im-* A: not able to occur
4. *mis-* D: an error
5. *pre-* B: before written records

Suffixes

1. *-ly;* A: in the right manner.
2. *-ful;* B: feeling or causing happiness
3. *-ist;* C: a person who studies science
4. *-ian;* D: a person who plays music
5. *-ment;* A: a feeling of eagerness

Writing

Nebraska Pioneer Children

1. Answers will vary.

2. Answers will vary, but should include: no electricity, food for survival, farmers were poor, so they could not afford to hire adult helpers, etc.

3. Answers will vary.

4. Boys: planting and harvesting, hunting and fishing, gathering fuel for the fire. Girls: cooking and cleaning, mending clothing, taking care of children. Answers might include physical strength, societal pressures, preparation for having a farm/husband/wife of their own one day.

The Olympics, Past and Present

1. Answers should include such elements as: Ancient were men only, they were summer only, they were conducted nude, games only included track and field type games, and they were a religious celebration. Modern are men and women, athletes wear clothing, there are MANY more events and games, they are both summer and winter.

2. Answers will vary.

3. Answers will vary.

4. Answers will vary.

Language

Language Answer Key

Prepositions

1. between
2. over
3. across
4. toward
5. around

Conjunctions

1. and - coordinating
2. because - subordinating
3. Neither/nor - correlative
4. although - subordinating
5. not only / but also - correlative
6. but - subordinating
7. and - coordinating
8. Either / or - correlative
9. unless - subordinating
10. Both / and - correlative

Verb Tenses

1. will go - C
2. cooks - A
3. rained - B
4. will visit - C
5. lives - A
6. rode
7. enjoys
8. will read
9. wanted
10. will play

Capitalization

1. Yes
2. Yes
3. No
4. Yes
5. Yes
6. No
7. Yes
8. Yes

Ending Punctuation

1. Question mark (?)
2. Period (.)
3. Period (.)
4. Exclamation point (!)
5. Question mark (?)
6. Exclamation point (!)
7. Question mark (?)
8. Period (.)
9. Question mark (?)
10. Exclamation point (!)

Commas

1. In Houston, Texas, there is a huge rodeo in February.
2. Johnny said, "Let's go play on the swings."
3. It's going to rain today, isn't it?
4. Nate had three apples, two oranges, and a banana in his lunch box.
5. Eureka, a show on the SyFy channel, is about a town of geniuses.
6. The Revolutionary War officially ended on May 12, 1784.
7. Yes, thank you, I would love some cake.
8. Along with his friends, Evan thought he could help others.
9. Because of the lightning, we could not play outside.
10. We can vacation at the beach, or we can go to the city.
11. & 12. Answers will vary

Titles

1. To Kill A Mockingbird is my favorite novel.
2. The headline read, "Man Kills Seven in Subway."
3. My class went to see "An Ideal Husband," a play by Oscar Wilde.
4. The Avengers was the best movie this summer!
5. "What Sarah Said," by Death Cab for Cutie, is the best song ever.

Changing Sentences

1. Nate and Evan go to the Houston Zoo on Sundays.
2. Dragonflies live by the river, where I hope to see some today.
3. Evan likes the monkeys that live in the primate habitat.
4. Baboons are from African and Asia, but they mostly live in zoos now.
5. Nick watches the baby giraffe as it tries to eat leaves from a tall tree.

Homophones

1. two
2. right
3. there
4. one
5. threw
6. err
7. aisle
8. ate
9. bass
10. bare

Heteronyms

1. The Polish furniture needs polish. (a substance to give a shiny surface)
2. I object to that object. (disapprove)
3. She was too close to the window to close it. (to shut)
4. The bass drum had a bass painted on it. (a fish)
5. Mr. Jones is ready to present the present to the President. (to give formally)
6. Don't desert us just because we are in the desert. (to leave)

7. The dove dove for the food. (a bird)
8. Give me a minute and I'll show you minute particles in my microscope. (tiny)
9. The singer is here to record a new record. (to preserve in sound)
10. I refuse to take out the refuse. (to say no)

Greek / Latin

1. A. photogenic
   B. photograph
   C. telephoto
   D. photosynthesis

2. A. aerodynamics
   B. aerobics
   C. aerate
   D. aeronautics

3. A. epidemic
   B. democracy
   C. demographic
   D. endemic

Context Clues

1. A - moved
2. B - get rid of
3. D - denied
4. A - huge
5. C - calm

Reference Materials

1. B - (2) /ˈmin(ē)əCHər/
2. C - (3)adj. of a much smaller size than normal
   noun. a thing that is much smaller than normal
   verb. represent on a smaller scale

3. D - (4)synonyms: diminutive, tiny, small
4. A - (1) Min-i-a-ture
5. D - Encyclopedia
6. A - Dictionary
7. C - Thesaurus
8. B - Glossary

Figurative language

1. A - simile
2. D - onomatopoeia
3. E - idiom
4. B - metaphor
5. C - alliteration

Synonyms

1. big
2. hard
3. bucket
4. mad
5. talk

Antonyms

6. city
7. full
8. beautiful / pretty
9. thaw
10. catch

Practice Test Answers

Practice Test #1

Answers and Explanations

1. Part A: D: The main objective of these paragraphs is to describe Manolo's and Barry's neighborhood.

Part B: There are several sentences that can be used here. Any one that describes their neighborhood is acceptable. For example, "There are no cypresses or any other kinds of trees in Cypress Heights."

2. A: The strange thing about the name of Barry's and Manolo's neighborhood is that there are no Cypress trees and the land is flat.

3. A: The first sentence shows that Cypress Heights residents do everything in their control (painting their houses and decorating their lawns) to make their places look nice.

4. A: Barry and Manolo like living close to each other because it makes it convenient for them to visit each other.

5. C: Plants that can live in very dry climates are called drought-resistant.

6. D: Mrs. Juarez put gravel on her lawn instead of grass. She used gravel because she wouldn't have to water it.

7. B: Traditionally, new neighbors receive gifts, not give them. That is why Barry asked Mrs. Juarez that question.

8. A: Knit in this case means to join together tightly.

9. B: Thomas wanted to replace a doll he bought for his sister, which broke before the warranty was up.

10. A: The warranty or guarantee for the doll was for one year.

11. C: The word "defective" is another way of saying "broken."

12. D: The company agreed to send Thomas a replacement doll after he sent in some paperwork.

13. B: Romco asked Thomas to fill out a form and send it to them.

14. III & V: Remember that facts can be proven, but someone's opinion is debatable. Both of these statements can be debated.

15. D: The correct form for writing the name of a town and state is Anywhere, Texas.

16. A: Romco did not have time to write an individual letter to all of the customers with complaints, so they wrote a general letter to all people who complained.

17. D: It took nine days for Romco to reply to Thomas's letter according to the dates on the letters.

18. B: The tone in both letters is polite.

19. B: Hobie chose baseball because his brother was already running track and he didn't want to be compared to him.

20. A: Twinge also means to hurt. Hobie flexed his leg so fast that it made his knee hurt a little.

21. D: Always being the first one to cross the finish line is a good indication that Hobie was (and still is) a good runner.

22. A: While Martin and Hobie may be different in many ways, they are both good at running.

23. C: Hobie had a hard decision to make. Forced to give up baseball, he had to choose between playing a sport where he might be compared to his brother or staying at home. Hobie found out that difficult decisions sometimes turn out all right in the end.

24. D: The author's step-by-step account of how Hobie made it from third to first place in the race increased the tension or suspense in the story.

25. A good summary of this story would be:

"Despite showing a talent for running, Hobie chose to play baseball to avoid comparisons to his older brother. His father's accident forced him to join track, where he did well."

26. C: Hobie's breathing became ragged because he was worn out from running so fast for so long.

27. C: Hobie is most likely to rejoin track the following year as a long-distance runner, an area where he showed talent. It will also allow him to avoid comparisons to his brother, who is a sprinter.

28. Part A: B: In the story it says, "While the crack of the starting gun was still ringing in his ears," which lets you know that it was the sound of the gun.

Part B: Knowing that is was the sound of the gun the only answer that makes sense is "snap".

29. C: The author started the story with the phrase "News flash" to attract the readers' attention. The article is about a scientific fact. It is not a breaking news story.

30. B: Cohesion is a kind of stickiness in which molecules stick to each other via attraction, much in the same way a magnet sticks to metal.

31. D: The point of the experiment is to see how many pennies it takes for an already full glass of water to overflow. That is why the glass must be in a clean, dry place.

32. A: Water is sticky because its molecules stick to each other.

33. C: A paper clip can float on top of water because the molecules are stuck together and can hold it up.

34. A: The three states of water are solid, liquid, and gas.

35. C: 186.4°F is the boiling point of water at 14,000 feet.

36. D: These sentences are both facts and can be proven.

37. C: In the article it states, "Here is another fun fact about water. When it is in its solid form, ice, it is less dense."

38. A: Both articles note that water is a unique substance.

39. B: The first article talks about a property of water (its stickiness) and the second article talks about a problem related to water (pollution).

40. D: Articles about the properties of water are most likely to be found in a science text.

Practice Test #2

Answers and Explanations

1. B: The expression "rain came down in sheets" means it was raining so hard that the rain looked like it was coming down in one solid sheet rather than separate drops.

2. D: Mona and Yuri's mother was asleep after having worked overnight as a nurse.

3. C: Mona and Yuri's mother goes to bed around 7 a.m. after working all night. She usually gets up after eight hours of sleep, which would be around 3 p.m.

4. A: War is a card game. It can be played with an ordinary deck of playing cards.

5. A: When a regular deck of playing cards is used, an ace has the highest value in War and beats all other cards.

6. B: To have a "war" in the card game War, both players have to have the same card.

7. C: Mona won the first game that she and Yuri played. That is why Yuri said, "Beginner's luck."

8. A: When she said, "Actually, this game is all luck," Mona meant that the game did not require any skill to win. It just depended on the cards the players had.

9. A: Mona wins the round. A king is the second highest card in the deck. A jack is the fourth highest.

10. C: Gov. Richards taught social studies and history before getting into politics.

11. Part A: D: Paragraph 3 is mostly about Gov. Richards's achievements as governor of Texas.

Part B: A: This is the only answer choice that states one of her achievements from paragraph 3.

12. B: The word "styled" refers to how her hair was fixed.

13. A: Gov. Richards was joking about how stiff her hair was because of all the hairspray in it.

14. Part A: C: Sen. Hutchinson earned a law degree from the University of Texas in 1967.

Part B: D: The second sentence in paragraph 1 reads, "She went to the University of Texas and graduated with a law degree in 1967."

15. B: Sen. Hutchinson worked as a TV news reporter before going into politics.

16. Part A: D: Paragraph 3 is mostly about Sen. Hutchinson's accomplishments while serving as a senator.

Part B: There are several examples that could be used here. Two of them are, "She worked to fix laws that changed the way money was spent for the military. She also wrote and helped pass a law that regulated shipping on the oceans."

17. A: The abbreviation Sen. means Senator.

18. B: Gov. Richards and Sen. Hutchinson were the first women to be governor and a U.S. senator in Texas.

19. C: Both women served as the Texas State Treasurer before getting more important positions in government.

20. B: Sen. Hutchinson is still working as a U.S. Senator. Gov. Richards died in 2006, and the passage states that she left politics.

21. A: The author wrote these articles to show that women can have the same opportunities as men in Texas.

22. B: Sam called Pavarti to get directions to Pavarti's house. Sam will give the directions to her mother when they drive over the next day.

23. A: Pavarti asked Sam where she lived so that she could give Sam directions from her own house.

24. D: Sam's mother will need to turn onto Elm Street after Townline Road.

25. A: Pavarti told Sam the color of her house and the houses around it because her address is hard to see from the road.

26. A: Sam's mother should go straight on Rio Turnpike before taking a right on Main Street.

27. C: Pavarti said to**, "**Look for either a red truck or a small black car."

28. B: Sam is hoping that her and her mother don't get lost and have to drive up and down Main Street, especially since it runs only one way.

29. D: Sam's notes written out would look like the following: *At the third traffic light you will turn left onto Rio Turnpike. Go about half a mile until you see a 7-Eleven on the right. The next street after the 7-Eleven is Main Street.*

30. D: After buying the pumpkins, Pavarti's family is planning to have lunch before starting to carve them.

31. Part A: C: Pedro noticed the model of the 1969 Mustang because his father had talked about that type of car.

Part B: B: In the story Pedro says that his grandfather had owned a real 1969 Mustang.

32. A: Simon wanted to buy a model of a C17 fighter plane, but he didn't have enough money.

33. B: Altogether, with tax, Simon had to pay $27.

34. C: After buying Simon's model, the B17G Flying Fortress, they planned to build it and then go buy the 1969 Mustang that Pedro wanted and build that one as well.

35. D: Simon turned down his father's offer of help, but accepted Pedro's.

36. Part A: B: It is likely that Simon will invite Pedro over to help the next time he builds a model airplane.

Part B: A: This is the sentence where he says that he will probably invite Pedro over to help.

37. D: The passage gives a strong indication that Simon and Pedro are friends.

38. A: Simon lets his father drive him and Pedro to the store to buy Pedro's model of a 1969 Mustang.

39. D: Simon learned from his father that he understands that Simon is growing up and relying less on his parents and more on his friends for help.

40. C: Simon accepts a drive from his father because traffic is heavier in the afternoon than it is in the morning.

Online Resources

Due to our efforts to try to keep this book to a manageable length, we've created a link that will give you access to all of your online resources:

mometrix.com/resources719/ssncg5elarwb

It's Your Moment, Let's Celebrate It!

Share your story @mometrixtestpreparation